D1006732

tea time

NEW
HOLLAND

contents

introduction

Western cultures tend to separate tea into those drinks made with the tea plant, and those we call herbal infusions. The earliest recorded tea usage was in 350 AD, when a Chinese dictionary cited tea for the first time as 'Erh Ya'.

Camellia sinensis: the tea plant

The leaves of tea from this plant is the world's most popular beverage, and yet no one thinks of tea in its many forms as a herb, even though it has been used in Chinese medicine for 5000 years! The dried leaves are the most popular variety amongst Western drinkers. Perhaps this is because black tea blends are more suited to the addition of milk and sugar.

Chinese leaves produce Keemun, Lapsang Souchong, Oolong and Yunnan teas. Most Chinese tea drinkers do not add milk or sugar.

In India, the best-known teas are Darjeeling, Assam and Nilgiri. Ceylon is a light tea with crisp citrus undertones.

The most common blended black teas for Western drinkers include English Breakfast, Earl Grey and Irish Breakfast.

Chai is popular also, and is black tea that is brewed strong with a combination of spices and diluted with milk and sugar.

Herbal infusions are comprised of fresh or dried herbs, spices, roots, seeds or flowers that are infused in hot water. Most herbal infusions are caffeine free.

tea

Bergamot earl grey spicy tea

1. Pour 1 cup of boiling water over Ceylon tea bag and 2 bergamot leaves, 1 cinnamon stick and 1 lemon slice. Remove the tea bag after 10–15 seconds. Stand for 5 minutes and stir frequently with the cinnamon stick. Strain, pour into a pretty mug, and add a sprinkling of cinnamon powder, a fresh lemon slice and a touch of honey.

1 Earl Grey tea bag
2 bergamot leaves
1 cinnamon stick
cinnamon powder
2 fresh lemon slice
honey to taste

Authentic jasmine tea

1. Dry the jasmine flowers on brown paper in the shade or on a stainless steel table. When almost dry, add to green tea or ordinary Ceylon tea in the ratio of 1 cup of flowers to 4 cups of tea. Place in a large tin. Shake them up daily.

2. Now add ¼ cup of flowers and green tea mixture to 1 cup of boiling water with cloves. Stand for 3–5 minutes, stir often. Strain. Add lemon juice, a little grated lemon zest and honey. Stir well. Sip slowly.

3. Avoid during pregnancy.

1 cup of jasmine flowers
4 cups of green or Ceylon tea
3 cloves
juice of ½ lemon
grated lemon zest
1 teaspoon honey

Lavender tea

2-3 sprigs lavender
3 thin slices of ginger root
1 teaspoon of honey
3 cardamom pods

1. Take 2–3 sprigs (or enough to fill ¼ of a cup) of lavender. Pour over this 1 cup of boiling water, add ginger root, honey and cardamom pods. Crush well with a spoon. Stand for 5 minutes, strain and sip slowly, preferably while lying in a bath fragrant with fresh lavender hung under the tap, lavender soap and bath oil and a lavender scented candle, and relax.

Classic chamomile

¼ cup of fresh or less of dried
  chamomile flowers
thumb-length sprig of lemon balm
3 allspice berries, lightly cracked
a little honey

1.   Cover chamomile flowers with 1 cup of boiling water. Add lemon balm and allspice berries. Stand for 5 minutes. Strain. Add honey to sweeten and stir well. Sip slowly and feel the tension melt away.

Rooibos health tea

1. Take rooibos, fresh lemon and lemon juice, fresh ginger, cloves and lemon balm or spearmint. Pour 2 cups of boiling water over everything, stand for 5 minutes, strain. Sweeten with a touch of honey. Pour 1 cup hot tea, sip slowly and keep the rest in the fridge for later and have it cold with ice.

1 teaspoon or 1 tea bag of rooibos
1 slice of fresh lemon and a good squeeze of lemon juice
3 thin slices of fresh ginger
3 cloves
2 sprigs of lemon balm leaves or a thumb-length sprig of spearmint

Raspberry iced tea

1. Take the large raspberry leaf with 6 raspberries, cinnamon and cloves, and pour 1 cup of boiling water over, add lemon zest and stir well. Stand for 5 minutes. Strain and cool. Now add 12 more raspberries, cucumber and fresh mint. Whirl in a liquidiser. Add ice. Serve chilled. It's refreshingly unusual and delicious! You can add honey if liked.

1 large raspberry leaf
18 raspberries
a stick of cinnamon
2 cloves
1 teaspoon of lemon zest
2 slices of cucumber
sprig of fresh mint

sandwiches

Dainty seafood circles

1. Combine mayonnaise, tomato sauce and Worcestershire Sauce. Season with salt and pepper. This mixture must be quite stiff, otherwise it will not coat the prawns and will make a soggy sandwich.

2. Add shrimp (prawns) and stir gently to coat.

3. Cut three circles out of each slice of bread using a 4cm (1½in) cookie cutter (serrated is best for a pretty edge).

4. Spread 2 teaspoons prawn mixture onto 15 circles. Sprinkle each with paprika.

5. Top with remaining fresh bread circles.

6. Arrange on a large platter, garnished with watercress or mustard cress.

2 tablespoons (30ml) mayonnaise
2 teaspoons (10ml) tomato
  sauce
a dash of Worcestershire Sauce
salt and black pepper
200g (6½oz) fresh, peeled and
  cooked shrimp (prawns)
  (roughly chopped, depending
  on the size)
10 slices of soft white sliced fresh
  bread, lightly buttered
½ teaspoon paprika
watercress or mustard cress, to
  garnish

Chicken & walnut

1. Mix the cream cheese and mayonnaise together. If a more liquid consistency is needed to coat the chicken, add a small quantity of milk.
2. Stir the walnuts into the mayonnaise mixture.
3. Add the shredded chicken and chopped parsley, and mix to combine. Season to taste.
4. Divide the mixture onto two slices of fresh bread and top with the other slices.
5. Trim crusts off sandwich and cut into three fingers, then cut each finger in half.

½ tablespoon (10g) cream cheese (softened)
½ tablespoon (10g) mayonnaise
1 tablespoon (20ml) milk
a handful of walnuts, finely chopped
½ poached chicken breast (approx 100g/3½oz), shredded
1 tablespoon flat-leaf parsley, chopped
salt and black pepper
4 slices soft wholemeal fresh bread, lightly buttered

Crab, chives & celery

MAKES 6

¼ stick celery, very finely
  chopped
½ tablespoon (15g) crème fraiche
2 garlic chives (or ordinary
  chives), finely chopped
70g (2½oz) crabmeat
salt and black pepper
4 slices soft white bread, lightly
  buttered

1. Mix the celery with the crème fraiche and chives.
2. Add the crabmeat, gently stirring to combine. Season well with salt and pepper.
3. Spread the mixture onto two slices of fresh bread.
4. Top with second slice of bread.
5. Trim the crusts and cut into three fingers, then cut each finger in half.

Pesto & cheese triangles

MAKES 16

2 round Turkish pide buns
2 tablespoons tube blended basil
3 tablespoons pine nuts
½ cup shredded mozzarella
   cheese
½ cup shredded parmesan
   cheese
canola oil spray

1. Mix the 2 cheeses together.
2. Split each bun in half and spread 2 of the 4 halves with the basil, sprinkle with pine nuts and top with the cheese mix. Top each with half a bun.
3. Preheat a sandwich press and spray the base plate with oil.
4. Place the buns on the hot base, close lid and cook for 4 minutes or until crisp, and remove.
5. Using a sharp knife, cut each bun into 8 triangles. Serve warm.

Smoked trout with lime

MAKES 8

1. Combine the cream cheese and mayonnaise.
2. Add the juice and grated peel of ½ lime. The mixture needs to be quite stiff, so do not add all the lime juice if this makes it runny.
3. Season with salt and pepper to taste.
4. Spread quite thickly onto two slices of fresh bread.
5. Top with slices of ocean trout and second slice of fresh bread.
6. Trim the crusts and cut each into four neat triangles.

1 tablespoon softened cream cheese
2 teaspoons (10ml) whole egg mayonnaise
½ lime
salt and black pepper
4 slices soft wholemeal fresh bread, lightly buttered
50–100g (1½–3½oz) smoked ocean trout

Smoked salmon & cucumber

MAKES 6

1. Combine the mayonnaise, chopped capers and dill and spread on the two slices of fresh bread.
2. Place the smoked salmon generously on top.
3. Overlap nine thin slices of cucumber until they are covering the salmon.
4. Season with freshly ground black pepper.
5. Top with second slice of fresh bread.
6. Trim crusts off sandwich and cut into three fingers, then cut each finger in half.

1 tablespoon (20ml) whole egg
   mayonnaise
2 teaspoons (approx. 16) baby
   capers, chopped
1 teaspoon chopped fresh dill
4 slices soft white fresh bread,
   lightly buttered
50–100g (1½–3½oz) smoked
   salmon (or smoked trout)
¼ small or English cucumber,
   finely sliced
black pepper

Smoked turkey open sandwich

MAKES 12

1 tablespoon (20ml) whole egg
   mayonnaise
12 slices (approx 200g/6½oz)
   smoked turkey
6 mini bagels, halved
salt and black pepper
2 tablespoons cranberry jelly
a handful of baby rocket leaves

1. Spread the mayonnaise evenly on each bagel half.
2. Put a slice of folded turkey on each bagel.
3. Season well with salt and black pepper.
4. Smear a teaspoon of cranberry jelly across the turkey.
5. Top with a few leaves of rocket (about 5 on each).
6. Serve on a large platter.

Egg and cress fingers

MAKES 6

2 hard boiled eggs
1 tablespoon (20ml) mayonnaise
salt and pepper
4 slices soft white fresh bread,
    lightly buttered
½ small punnet (approx
    100g/3½oz) mustard cress (or
    use finely shredded iceberg
    lettuce, watercress or snow
    pea sprouts)

1. Slice and fork the eggs together with mayonnaise, salt and pepper to make a coarse mixture.
2. Spread evenly across two slices of fresh bread.
3. Top one slice with scattered mustard cress and place other slice on top.
4. Trim crusts off sandwich and cut into three fingers, then cut each finger in half.

cupcakes

Butterfly cupcakes

1. Preheat oven to 200°C/400°F.

2. Beat butter, vanilla extract and sugar together in a bowl until light and fluffy. Add eggs one at a time, beating well after each addition.

3. Sift flour and salt together and add to creamed mixture alternately with milk. Stir until mixture is smooth and all ingredients are well combined.

4. Spoon about 1 tablespoon of mixture into each paper patty case or buttered patty pans. Bake in the oven for 15 minutes or until golden brown. Cool on a wire rack.

5. To make the filling, beat cream, vanilla extract and icing sugar together until thick.

6. When the cakes are cool, cut a slice from the top of each cake and spoon or pipe on a small amount of filling. Cut removed cake slices in half and arrange on top of cream to make butterfly wings. Dust with a little extra icing sugar and decorate with crystallised rose petals.

125g (4oz) butter or margarine
1 teaspoon vanilla extract
¾ cup superfine (caster) sugar
2 eggs
2 cups self-rising (self-raising) flour
pinch of salt
²/₃ cup milk

FILLING
1¼ cups thickened cream
½ teaspoon vanilla extract
2 tablespoons confectioners' (icing) sugar
crystallised rose petals
confectioners' (icing) sugar, extra

Coffee & hazelnut cupcakes

MAKES 12

1. Preheat the oven to 180°C/350°F. Line a 12-cupcake pan with cupcake papers. In a saucepan, heat the butter, milk and coffee gently and stir until butter is melted. Allow to cool.

2. In a large bowl, whisk the eggs with an electric mixer until thick and creamy. Add the sugar gradually, then stir in half the butter mixture and flour and beat. Add the remaining butter mixture and flour and beat until smooth.

3. Divide the mixture evenly between the cake papers. Bake for 20 minutes until risen and firm to touch. Allow to cool for a few minutes and then transfer to a wire rack. Allow to cool fully before icing.

TOPPING

1. Meanwhile, combine all of the ingredients in a medium-sized bowl and beat slowly with an electric mixer for 1 minute. Turn speed up and beat until light and fluffy.

2. Place mixture into a piping bag and pipe onto cupcakes, sprinkle with hazelnuts and dust with icing sugar and cocoa powder.

125g (4oz) butter, softened
½ cup milk
½ tablespoon instant coffee
2 eggs
1 cup superfine (caster) sugar
2 cups self-rising (self-raising) flour
½ cup chopped hazelnuts

TOPPING

1½ cups confectioners' (icing) sugar
2 tablespoons instant coffee
125g (4oz) butter, softened
4 drops vanilla extract
chopped toasted hazelnuts to decorate
confectioners' (icing) sugar and cocoa powder, for dusting

Pecan praline cupcakes

MAKES 12

2 eggs
125g (4oz) butter, softened
1 cup superfine (caster) sugar
½ cup milk
2 cups self-rising (self-raising)
    flour, sifted
1 tablespoon espresso coffee
½ cup pecans, chopped
1 tablespoon golden syrup

TOPPING
1½ cups confectioners' (icing)
    sugar
125g (4oz) butter, softened
200g (7oz) sugar
100ml (3½fl oz) water
100g (3½oz) pecans, chopped

1.   Preheat the oven to 160°C/325°F. Line a 12-cupcake pan with cupcake papers. In a medium-sized bowl, lightly beat the eggs, add butter and sugar, then mix until light and fluffy.
2.   Add milk and flour, and stir to combine. Add remaining ingredients. Mix with a wooden spoon for 2 minutes, until light and creamy.
3.   Divide the mixture evenly between the cake papers. Bake for 18–20 minutes until risen and firm to touch. Allow to cool for a few minutes, then transfer to a wire rack. Allow to cool fully before icing.

TOPPING
1.   Meanwhile, combine sugar, butter and 100ml water in a saucepan, bring to the boil and simmer over a medium heat until the mixture becomes a golden colour. Stir in pecans and quickly pour onto an oiled tray. Allow to cool and harden before breaking into pieces.
2.   Beat together icing sugar and butter until light and fluffy. Use a piping bag fitted with a plain nozzle and pipe the icing onto the cupcakes. Decorate with praline pieces.

Malted milk mini cupcakes

MAKES 24

80g (3oz) butter, softened
½ cup superfine (caster) sugar
1 egg
1 tablespoon cocoa powder,
    sifted
1 cup self-rising (self-raising)
    flour, sifted
½ cup milk
½ teaspoon vanilla extract

TOPPING
80g (3oz) butter, softened
1 cup confectioners' (icing) sugar
2 tablespoons malted milk
    powder
24 chocolate covered malt balls

1. Preheat the oven to 160°C/325°F. Line a 24 mini cupcake pan with mini cupcake papers. In a medium sized bowl, use an electric mixer on high speed to cream the butter and sugar until light and fluffy. Add the egg and mix well.

2. Add the cocoa, flour, milk and vanilla, and beat with an electric mixer on medium until well combined.

3. Divide the mixture evenly between the 24 mini cupcake papers. Bake for 10–15 minutes until well risen and firm to the touch. Allow to cool for a few minutes and then transfer to a wire rack. Allow to cool fully before icing.

TOPPING

1. Use an electric mixer on high speed to beat the butter and malted milk powder, until light and fluffy. Gradually beat in icing sugar until all combined, continue beating for 1 minute. Place mixture into a piping bag with a plain nozzle and pipe onto cupcakes. Decorate with chocolate malt balls.

Dark choc truffle cupcakes

MAKES 12

1. Preheat the oven to 160°C/325°F. Line a 12-cupcake pan with cupcake papers. In a medium-sized bowl, lightly beat the eggs, add butter and sugar, then mix until light and fluffy.
2. Add yoghurt, flour and vanilla, and stir to combine. Add remaining ingredients. Beat with an electric mixer for 2 minutes, until light and creamy.
3. Divide the mixture evenly between the cake papers. Bake for 18–20 minutes until risen and firm to touch. Allow to cool for a few minutes, and then transfer to a wire rack. Allow to cool fully before icing.

TOPPING
1. Meanwhile, combine the chocolate and butter in a medium-sized saucepan over a medium heat. As the mixture begins to melt, reduce heat to low, stirring constantly, until melted. Remove from heat, add cream, and stir. Rest for 10 minutes: the mixture will be firm and velvety in consistency.
2. Use a piping bag fitted with a star nozzle pipe the mixture onto the cupcakes. Dust heavily with cocoa.

2 eggs
125g (4oz) butter, softened
1 cup superfine (caster) sugar
½ cup vanilla-flavoured yoghurt
2 cups self-rising (self-raising)
*   flour, sifted*
1 tablespoon vanilla extract
100g dark chocolate pieces
1 tablespoon cocoa powder

TOPPING
100g (3oz) dark chocolate pieces
20g (¾oz) butter, softened
¹/₃ cup thickened cream
cocoa for dusting

Raspberry cupcakes

MAKES 12

1. Preheat the oven to 160°C/325°F. Line a 12-cupcake pan with cupcake papers. In a medium-sized bowl, lightly beat the eggs, add butter and sugar, then mix until light and fluffy.
2. Add milk, flour and vanilla, and stir to combine. Beat with an electric mixer for 2 minutes, until light and creamy. Stir in crushed raspberries.
3. Divide the mixture evenly between the cake papers. Bake for 18–20 minutes until risen and firm to touch. Allow to cool for a few minutes and then transfer to a wire rack. Allow to cool fully before icing.

TOPPING

1. Meanwhile, combine confectioners' (icing) sugar and butter in a small bowl, mix with a wooden spoon until well combined, then beat with a whisk until light and fluffy.
2. Spoon mixture into a piping bag with a medium-sized star shaped nozzle. Pipe icing onto each cupcake and decorate with the sugared raspberries. Serve immediately.
3. To sugar the raspberries, brush with lightly beaten eggwhites and dust with caster sugar.

2 eggs
125g (4oz) butter, softened
1 cup superfine (caster) sugar
½ cup milk
2 cups self-rising (self-raising) flour, sifted
1 teaspoon vanilla extract
¼ cup raspberries, crushed

TOPPING
1½ cups confectioners' (icing) sugar
125g (4oz) butter, softened
sugared raspberries

Choc strawberry mini cupcakes

MAKES 24

125g (4oz) butter, softened
1 cup superfine (caster) sugar
2 eggs
2 cups self-rising (self-raising)
   flour, sifted
2 tablespoons cocoa, sifted
½ cup milk
½ cup strawberries and chopped

TOPPING
1 cup cream, whipped
strawberries, sliced, to decorate
dark chocolate, grated, to
   decorate

1.   Preheat the oven to 160°C/325°F. Line a 24 mini cupcake pan with mini cupcake papers. In a medium sized bowl, use an electric mixer on high speed to cream the butter and sugar until light and fluffy. Add the egg and mix well.

2.   Add the flour, milk and cocoa, and beat with an electric mixer on medium until well combined. Stir in strawberries.

3.   Divide the mixture evenly between the 24 mini cupcake papers. Bake for 10–15 minutes until well risen and firm to the touch. Allow to cool for a few minutes and then transfer to a wire rack. Allow to cool fully before icing.

TOPPING

1.   Top the cupcakes with whipped cream and decorate with strawberries and grated dark chocolate.

Lemon poppy cupcakes

MAKES 12

2 eggs
125g (4oz) butter, softened
1 cup superfine (caster) sugar
½ cup Greek-style yoghurt
2 cups self-rising (self-raising)
   flour, sifted
zest of 2 lemons
juice of 1 lemon
1 teaspoon poppy seeds

TOPPING
1½ cups confectioners' (icing)
   sugar
125g (4oz) butter, softened
juice of 1 lemon
½ teaspoon poppy seeds
zest of 1 lemon
50g (1¾oz) candied lemon, cut
   into thin slivers

1.   Preheat the oven to 160°C/325°F. Line a 12-cupcake pan with cupcake papers. In a medium-sized bowl, lightly beat the eggs, add butter and sugar, then mix until light and fluffy.

2.   Add yoghurt and flour, and stir to combine. Beat with an electric mixer for 2 minutes, until light and creamy. Stir through lemon zest, lemon juice and poppy seeds.

3.   Divide the mixture evenly between the cake cases. Bake for 18–20 minutes until risen and firm to touch. Allow to cool for a few minutes and then transfer to a wire rack. Allow to cool fully before icing.

TOPPING
1.   Meanwhile, combine all the topping ingredients except the candied lemon, mix and spoon onto cakes. Top with candied lemon pieces.

Vanilla rose petal cupcakes

MAKES 12

1. Preheat the oven to 160°C/325°F. Line a 12-cupcake pan with cupcake papers. In a medium-sized bowl, lightly beat the eggs, add butter and sugar, then mix until light and fluffy.

2. Add milk, flour and vanilla, and stir to combine. Beat with an electric mixer for 2 minutes, until light and creamy.

3. Divide the mixture evenly between the cake papers. Bake for 18–20 minutes until risen and firm to touch. Allow to cool for a few minutes and then transfer to a wire rack. Allow to cool fully before icing.

TOPPING

1. Meanwhile, combine half of all the topping ingredients except roses, mix with a wooden spoon, add remaining ingredients and beat with the spoon until light and fluffy.

2. Place mixture into a piping bag with a plain nozzle and pipe onto cupcakes. Decorate with rose petals.

2 eggs
125g (4oz) butter, softened
1 cup superfine (caster) sugar
½ cup milk
2 cups self-rising (self-raising)
   flour, sifted
1 teaspoon vanilla extract

TOPPING

1½ cups confectioners' (icing)
   sugar
1 teaspoon rose water
125g (4oz) butter, softened
6 drops vanilla extract
candied rose petals (available
   from cake decoration stores)

Apple tea cakes

1. Preheat oven to 200°C/400°F.
2. Sift together the self-raising flour, salt, cinnamon and nutmeg. Cream butter and sugar until light and fluffy, add egg and beat well. Fold in the sifted dry ingredients alternately with the peeled apple slices and sufficient milk to make a dropping consistency.
3. Spoon mixture into paper-lined deep patty pans. Top with unpeeled apple slices. Sprinkle each with a little extra sugar and cinnamon. Bake in the upper half of the oven for 15–20 minutes. Serve with butter.

2 cups self-rising (self-raising) flour
½ teaspoon salt
½ teaspoon ground cinnamon
½ teaspoon ground nutmeg
60g (2oz) butter
½ cup superfine (caster) sugar
1 egg, lightly beaten
1 apple, peeled and finely diced
¾ cup milk
extra sugar and cinnamon
1 apple, unpeeled, finely sliced

Hazelnut express

MAKES 12

3 eggs
180g (6oz) butter, softened
1 cup superfine (caster) sugar
½ cup milk
1 cup self-rising (self-raising)
   flour, sifted
¼ teaspoon baking powder
½ cup hazelnut meal
½ cup hazelnuts, chopped
½ cup cocoa powder
2 tablespoons instant coffee
   powder

TOPPING

1 cup confectioners' (icing) sugar
90g (3oz) unsalted butter
1 tablespoon hazelnut liqueur
12 coffee beans

1. Preheat the oven to 160°C/325°F. Line a 12-cupcake pan with cupcake papers. In a medium-sized bowl, lightly beat the eggs, add butter and sugar, then mix until light and fluffy.

2. Add milk and flour, and stir to combine. Add remaining cupcake ingredients. Mix with a wooden spoon for 2 minutes, until light and creamy.

3. Divide the mixture evenly between the cake papers. Bake for 18–20 minutes until risen and firm to touch. Allow to cool for a few minutes and then transfer to a wire rack. Allow to cool fully before icing.

4. To make the topping, combine all topping ingredients except for coffee beans in a small bowl, mix with a wooden spoon, and spoon onto cupcakes. Decorate each cake with a coffee bean.

cakes

Raspberry chocolate truffle cakes

MAKES 8

1. Preheat oven to 180°C/350°F.
2. Combine cocoa powder and 1 cup boiling water. Mix to dissolve and set aside to cool.
3. Place butter and sugar in a bowl and beat until light and fluffy. Beat in eggs, one at a time, adding a little flour with each egg. Fold remaining flour and cocoa mixture, alternately, into creamed butter mixture. Spoon mixture into eight lightly buttered 1/2-cup capacity ramekins or large muffin tins. Bake for 20–25 minutes or until cakes are cooked when tested with a skewer. Cool for 5 minutes, then turn onto wire racks to cool. Turn cakes upside down and scoop out centre, leaving a 12mm (1/2in) shell. Spread each cake with chocolate to cover top and sides, then place right way up on a wire rack.
4. To make cream, fold raspberry purée into cream. Spoon cream into a piping bag fitted with a large nozzle. Carefully turn cakes upside down and pipe in cream to fill cavity. Place right way up on individual serving plates. Garnish with fresh raspberries.

½ cup cocoa powder, sifted
125g (4oz) butter
1¾ cups superfine (caster) sugar
2 eggs
1⅔ cups self-rising (self-raising) flour, sifted
400g (14oz) dark chocolate, melted
fresh raspberries

RASPBERRY CREAM
125g (4oz) raspberries, puréed and sieved
½ cup thickened cream, whipped

Cherry almond cake

SERVES 12

1.   Preheat oven to 180°C/350°F.

2.   Beat butter until soft, add sugar and continue beating until light and fluffy. Add eggs one at a time, beating well after each addition.

3.   Sift flour, cinnamon, cloves and ground almonds together. Add to creamed mixture with gin, mixing with a wooden spoon until ingredients are well combined.

4.   Spoon half the cake mixture into an 20cm (8in) round deep cake tin that has been base-lined with buttered baking paper. Spread evenly with 3 tablespoons of the jam, then spread evenly with remaining cake mixture.

5.   Bake for 1 hour or until pale golden. Cool in the tin for 5 minutes, then turn out onto a wire rack to cool. Spread top of cake with cream and decorate with remaining jam.

250g (8oz) butter or margarine
1 cup superfine (caster) sugar
2 eggs
2 cups plain flour
½ teaspoon ground cinnamon
½ teaspoon ground cloves
250g (8oz) ground almonds
1 tablespoon gin
5 tablespoons cherry jam
1 cup whipped cream

Strawberry hazelnut torte

SERVES 12

5 eggs
½ cup sugar
4 tablespoons plain flour
1 teaspoon coffee powder
1 teaspoon ground allspice
90g (3oz) ground hazelnuts

FILLING AND TOPPING
20 whole hazelnuts
150g (5oz) chocolate, melted
    with 60g (2oz) copha
2 cups thickened cream
4 tablespoons brandy
½ cup confectioners' (icing)
    sugar, sifted
2 punnets strawberries, sliced

1. Preheat oven to 180°C/350°F.
Beat eggs until light and fluffy, gradually
add sugar, beating well between each
addition. Sift together the flour, coffee
powder and allspice. Fold hazelnuts and
sifted ingredients gently into egg mixture.
Pour evenly into two square, well buttered
and lined 23cm (9in) sandwich tins.
2. Bake in the centre of the oven for
10–15 minutes. Remove from oven, cool,
then replace in oven for a further 5 minutes.
Cut tortes in half to form four oblong layers.
3. To make the filling and topping, dip
hazelnuts into chocolate mixture and allow
to set. Spread remaining chocolate evenly
over three torte layers.
4. Whip together the cream, brandy and
icing sugar. Add the strawberries to half the
cream mixture. Mix thoroughly and spread
onto the three chocolate covered layers.
Place these layers on top of each other,
finishing with the uncovered layer. Spread
remaining cream over the assembled torte
and decorate with cream, chocolate
hazelnuts and extra strawberries.
Refrigerate for 2 hours before serving.

Chocolate fudge torte

SERVES 8

90g (3oz) butter
150g (5oz) superfine (caster)
  sugar
5 eggs, separated
75g (2½oz) dark chocolate,
  melted
2 tablespoons brandy
90g (3oz) ground almonds
45g (1½oz) fresh white
  breadcrumbs

TOPPING
125g (4oz) dark Toblerone,
  melted
2 tablespoons dark corn syrup
15g (½oz) butter, melted
1 tablespoon cream

1. Preheat oven to 180°C/350°F.
2. Beat butter and sugar together until
pale and creamy. Beat in the egg yolks one
at a time, then beat in melted chocolate and
brandy. Fold in the ground almonds and
breadcrumbs, mix well.
Beat egg whites until soft peaks form,
fold into chocolate mixture in two batches.
Pour into a baking paper-lined and flour
dusted 23cm (9in) springform tin. Bake for
30–35 minutes. Turn out onto a wire rack to
cool.
3. To make the topping, combine
Toblerone, corn syrup, butter and cream in
a small saucepan over low heat, stir until
combined. Spread over cooled cake.

Pear upside down cake

SERVES 8

1. Preheat oven to 180°C/350°F.
2. Sprinkle base of a buttered and lined, deep 23cm (9in) round cake tin with demerara sugar. Cut pear halves in half to form quarters and arrange cut-side up, over base.
3. Place butter, flour, sugar and eggs in a food processor and process until smooth. Stir in walnuts. Carefully spoon batter over fruit in tin and bake for 1–1¼ hours or until cooked when tested with a skewer.
4. Place maple syrup and reserved pear juice in a saucepan over a medium heat and cook until syrup is reduced by half.
5. Turn cake onto a serving plate and pour over syrup. Serve with cream or ice cream.

¼ cup demerara sugar
2 x 440g (15oz) canned pear halves, drained and 1 cup syrup reserved
250g (8oz) butter, softened
2 cups self-rising (self-raising) flour
1 cup superfine (caster) sugar
4 eggs
1 cup chopped walnuts
¼ cup maple syrup

Simnel cake

SERVES 12

250g (8oz) unsalted butter
grated zest of 2 lemons
1¼ cups superfine (caster) sugar
4 eggs, beaten
1 cup mixed peel
1 cup sultanas
4 cups currants
3½ cups plain flour
pinch of salt
½ teaspoon baking powder
2 teaspoons mixed spice
2 tablespoons milk
450g (16oz) prepared marzipan
  or almond paste
1 egg white, lightly beaten

1. Preheat oven to 180°C/350°F.

2. Cream butter with lemon zest and sugar until light and fluffy. Add eggs one at a time, beating well after each addition. Stir in the mixed peel, sultanas and currants.

3. Sift together flour, salt, baking powder and mixed spice. Fold into the creamed mixture. Add milk and fold through until thoroughly combined. Spoon into a buttered and brown paper-lined 20cm (8 in) deep round tin. Bake for 3½ hours. Allow cake to cool in the tin.

4. Knead marzipan or almond paste thoroughly until smooth. Divide in half, roll one half onto a board lightly dusted with icing sugar to form a circle 18cm (7in) round. Brush top of cake with the egg white, top with the round of marzipan and crimp the edge using your thumb and index finger. Shape remaining paste into 11 balls. Place balls around edge of top of cake. Tie a red ribbon around the cake, finishing with a big, pretty bow to decorate.

Muddy mud cake

SERVES 6

250g (8oz) butter, softened

250g (8oz) bittersweet chocolate, chopped

100g (31/2oz) superfine (caster) sugar

90g (3oz) brown sugar

1½ tablespoons brandy

200g (7oz) plain flour

1 teaspoon baking powder

3 tablespoons Dutch cocoa powder

2 eggs

1 teaspoon vanilla extract

HOT FUDGE SAUCE

1 cup white sugar

½ cup brown sugar

½ cup cocoa powder

2 tablespoons plain flour

¼ teaspoon salt

30g (1oz) butter

¼ teaspoon vanilla extract

¾ cup water

1. Preheat the oven to 150°C/300°F and butter a 24cm (9½in) non-stick springform cake tin, or small moulds.

2. In a saucepan, melt the butter, then add the chocolate, sugars, brandy and 1½ cups water. Mix well with a whisk until the mixture is smooth.

3. Sift together the flour, baking powder and cocoa and add to the chocolate mixture with the eggs and vanilla. Beat until just combined – don't worry if the mixture is lumpy.

4. Pour into the cake tin and bake for 50 minutes or, if using moulds, for 30 minutes. Allow to cool in the tin or moulds for 15 minutes, then turn out.

5. To make hot fudge sauce, mix dry ingredients in a medium saucepan and add butter and ¾ cup water. Bring to the boil and continue boiling for about 10 minutes. Remove from heat and add vanilla extract.

6. Dust cake with icing sugar and serve warm with cream or ice cream and hot fudge sauce.

Chocolate hazelnut cake

SERVES 8

1. Preheat the oven to 190°C/375°F. Place chocolate in a heatproof bowl set over a saucepan of simmering water and heat, stirring, until chocolate melts. Remove bowl from pan and cool slightly.
2. Place egg yolks and sugar in a bowl and beat until thick and pale. Fold chocolate, hazelnuts and rum into egg mixture.
3. Place egg whites into a clean bowl and beat until stiff peaks form. Fold egg whites into chocolate mixture. Pour mixture into a buttered and lined 23cm (9in) springform tin and bake for 50 minutes or until cooked when tested with a skewer. Cool cake in tin. Just prior to serving, dust cake with icing sugar.

TIP
To toast hazelnuts, place nuts on a baking tray and bake for 10 minutes or until skins begin to split. Place on a tea towel and rub to remove skins. Place in a food processor and process to roughly chop.

250g (9oz) dark chocolate,
*   broken into pieces*
6 eggs, separated
1 cup sugar
325g (11½oz) hazelnuts, toasted
*   and roughly chopped*
1 tablespoon rum
confectioners' (icing) sugar, for
*   dusting*

slices

Choc-mint brownies

1. Preheat oven to 160°C/325°F.
2. Melt butter and chocolate in a medium saucepan, stir until combined then cool slightly. Beat eggs and sugar until light and creamy. Beat in cocoa and oil, then beat in flour and cooled chocolate mixture.
3. Pour mixture into a buttered and lined 23 x 23cm (9 x 9in) square tin. Bake for 40 minutes or until cooked when tested with a skewer. Turn onto wire rack to cool.
4. To make the icing, sift icing sugar into a heatproof bowl, add butter and peppermint extract and stir over simmering water until smooth. Drizzle or pipe icing over top of brownies. Cut into squares and serve.

125g (4oz) butter
200g (7oz) dark chocolate, grated
2 eggs
¾ cup brown sugar
2 tablespoons cocoa powder
2 tablespoons oil
1 cup plain flour

ICING
1 cup confectioners' (icing) sugar
15g (½oz) butter
3 drops peppermint extract

Chocolate rum slice

MAKES 25

1. Preheat oven to 180°C/350°F. Place flour, cocoa powder, caster sugar, coconut and raisins in a bowl and mix to combine. Stir in butter, rum, grated chocolate and eggs. Mix well.

2. Press mixture into a buttered and lined 25cm (10 in) square cake tin and bake for 20–25 minutes or until firm. Allow to cool in tin.

3. To make icing, sift icing sugar and cocoa powder together into a bowl. Add butter and 1 tablespoon boiling water and beat to make icing of a spreadable consistency.

4. Turn slice onto a wire rack or plate, spread with icing and sprinkle with extra coconut. Refrigerate until icing is firm, then cut into squares.

1 cup self-rising (self-raising) flour, sifted
1 tablespoon cocoa powder, sifted
½ cup superfine (caster) sugar
75g (2½oz) desiccated coconut
75g (2½oz) raisins, chopped
125g (4oz) butter, melted
1 teaspoon rum
2 tablespoons grated dark chocolate
2 eggs, lightly beaten

CHOCOLATE ICING
1 cup confectioners' (icing) sugar
2 tablespoons cocoa powder
15g (½oz) butter, softened

Raspberry yoghurt slice

MAKES 15

100g (3½oz) butter
1 cup plain flour
¼ cup brown sugar
¾ cup rolled oats

TOPPING

125g (4 oz) cream cheese
¾ cup raspberry-flavoured
   yoghurt
1 tablespoon honey
1 teaspoon lemon juice
1 teaspoon grated lemon zest
1 tablespoon gelatine
250g (8oz) frozen raspberries
¼ cup sugar

1. Preheat oven to 180°C/350°F.
2. Blend butter and flour in a food processor with sugar until dough just comes together. Fold through the oats.
3. Press into the base of a buttered and lined 28 x 18cm (11 x 7in) lamington tin. Bake for about 15–20 minutes or until a skewer comes out clean, then allow to cool.
4. Beat the cream cheese with yoghurt and honey, add lemon juice and zest. Sprinkle gelatine over ¼ cup water to soften. Heat ¾ of the thawed raspberries in a saucepan and add sugar and softened gelatine. Bring to the boil, stirring until sugar and gelatine have thoroughly dissolved. Press through a sieve and allow to cool. Then stir into the creamed cheese and yoghurt mixture with the remaining raspberries.
5. Carefully pour the yoghurt mixture over the base and refrigerate overnight. Serve with extra raspberries.

Chocolate chip squares

MAKES 18

220g (7¾oz) butter, softened
200g (7oz) brown sugar
1 teaspoon vanilla extract
300g (10½oz) plain flour
200g (7oz) plain or milk
  chocolate chips or plain or
  milk chocolate, chopped into
  chunks

1. Preheat the oven to 180°C/350°F.
2. Lightly grease a 38 x 25cm
(15 x 10in) baking tin.
3. Beat the butter and sugar using
an electric mixer until light and fluffy,
about 5 minutes (the secret!). Beat in
the vanilla extract. Stir in the flour and
chocolate chips. Pat the dough into
the prepared baking tray. Bake for
25–28 minutes, until the edges are
slightly crispy. Allow to cool before
slicing into squares.

Date & hazelnut crumble slice

MAKES 16

1. Preheat the oven to 200°C/400°F and line an 18 x 27cm (7 x 10¾in) baking tin with baking parchment.

2. Put the filling ingredients in a saucepan and bring to the boil. Reduce the heat and simmer for 10–15 minutes, or until thick. Allow to cool.

3. Mix together the flour, caster sugar and baking powder for the base. Using your hands or a food processor, rub in the butter to resemble fine breadcrumbs. Press the mixture firmly into the tin and bake for 15–18 minutes, or until brown around the edges. Remove from the oven.

4. Combine the crumble ingredients together in another bowl until the mixture is crumbly. Spread the date mixture over the cooked base then sprinkle over the crumble mixture, pressing it down firmly but gently. Return to the oven and cook for a further 15–20 minutes, or until the crumble topping is golden. Allow to cool completely in the tin before serving or serve warm with a spoonful of vanilla ice cream.

FILLING
400g (14oz) dried stoned dates, roughly chopped
grated rind of 2 lemons
250ml (9fl oz) water
75g (2¾oz) sugar

BASE
225g (8oz) plain flour
100g (3½oz) superfine (caster) sugar
1 teaspoon baking powder
125g (4½oz) firm butter, cut into chunks

CRUMBLE TOPPING
100g (3½oz) plain flour
50g (1¾oz) light brown sugar
75g (2¾oz) hazelnuts, roughly chopped
75g (2¾oz) firm butter

Lemon & blueberry shortcake slice

MAKES 20

1. Preheat the oven to 180°C/350°F. Line the base and sides of an 18 x 27cm (7 x 10¾in) tin with baking parchment.

2. Put the flour and the first measure of sugar in a large bowl or food processor and mix to combine. Add the butter and rub together or process until the mixture resembles fine breadcrumbs. Press the crumbs evenly into the prepared tin and bake for 20–25 minutes, or until golden. Remove and reduce the temperature to 140°C/275°F.

3. While the base is cooking, whisk together the eggs and the second measure of sugar, using an electric mixer, until very thick and pale, about 8–10 minutes. Stir in the lemon juice and rind then fold in the flour. Sprinkle the blueberries evenly over the base, if using. Pour over the egg mixture and bake for 35–40 minutes, or until set. Allow to cool in the tin before cutting into bars. Serve dusted with icing sugar, if liked.

4. Try stirring fresh rather than dried blueberries into the lemon topping before baking.

BASE
225g (8oz) plain flour
100g (3½oz) superfine (caster) sugar
175g (6oz) firm butter, cut into cubes

TOPPING
3 eggs
225g (8oz) superfine (caster) sugar, for the base
juice (about 100ml/3½ oz) and grated rind of 3 lemons
40g (1½oz) flour
75g (2¾oz) dried blueberries (optional)
confectioners' (icing) sugar, to serve (optional)

Ginger crunch

MAKES 24

BASE

225g (8oz) plain flour
100g (3½oz) superfine (caster)
    sugar
1 teaspoon baking powder
2 teaspoons ground ginger
150g (5½oz) butter, cut into
    cubes

ICING

150g (5½oz) butter
60ml (2floz) golden syrup
300g (10½oz) confectioners'
    (icing) sugar, sifted
2 tablespoons ground ginger

1. Preheat the oven to 180°C/350°F. Line a deep-sided 18 x 27-cm (7 x 10¾in) shallow baking tin with baking parchment.
2. To make the base, put the flour, sugar, baking powder and ginger in a food processor. Pulse several times to combine then add the butter. Process for about 30 seconds, or until the mixture resembles fine breadcrumbs. This can also be done by hand. Press the mixture evenly into the tin and level off, using the back of a spoon.
3. Bake for 20–25 minutes, or until lightly golden. Remove from the oven and allow to cool completely.
4. To make the icing, put the butter and golden syrup in a medium saucepan and heat until just melted. Add the sifted icing sugar and ginger and cook for a further 1–2 minutes, stirring constantly until smooth. Remove from the heat and pour over the base. Leave to set. Remove from the tin and cut into squares or triangles to serve.

Caramel squares

MAKES 24

SHORTBREAD BASE
100g (3½oz) butter
3 tablespoons sugar
60g (2oz) cornflour, sifted
¾ cup plain flour, sifted

CARAMEL FILLING
125g (4oz) butter
½ cup brown sugar
2 tablespoons honey
400g (14oz) sweetened
*   condensed milk*
1 teaspoon vanilla extract

CHOCOLATE TOPPING
200g (7oz) dark chocolate,
*   melted*

1. Preheat oven to 180°C/350°F. To make base, place butter and sugar in a bowl and beat until light and fluffy. Mix in cornflour and flour, turn onto a lightly floured surface and knead briefly, then press into a buttered and lined 20 x 30cm (8 x 12in) shallow cake tin and bake for 25 minutes or until firm.

2. To make filling, place butter, brown sugar and honey in a saucepan and cook over a medium heat, stirring constantly until sugar melts and ingredients are combined. Bring to the boil and simmer for 7 minutes. Beat in condensed milk and vanilla extract, pour filling over base and bake for 20 minutes longer. Set aside to cool completely. Spread melted chocolate over filling, set aside until firm, then cut into squares.

scones
&
muffins

Butterscotch buns

MAKES 12

1. Preheat oven to 220°C/420°F. Cream softened butter and brown sugar together in a small bowl. Set aside.
2. In a large bowl, combine flour, sugar, baking powder and salt. Cut in chilled butter until crumbly. Make a well in the centre. Pour milk into the well. Stir to make a soft dough. Knead 8–10 times. Pat or roll out on lightly floured surface to 23–25cm (9–10in) square. Spread with brown sugar mixture.
3. Sprinkle with nuts. Roll up as for jelly roll. Pinch edge to seal. Cut into 12 slices. Place on buttered 20 x 20cm (8 x 8in) pan. Bake 15–20 minutes. Invert over tray while hot.

60g (2oz) butter, softened, plus 45g (1½oz) chilled
¾ cup brown sugar, packed
2 cups plain flour
2 tablespoons granulated sugar
4 teaspoons baking powder
1 teaspoon salt
¾ cup milk
⅓ cup chopped nuts

Traditional scones

MAKES 12

1. Preheat oven to 220°C/420°F.
2. Sift flour and baking powder into a large bowl. Stir in sugar, then rub in butter using fingertips until mixture resembles coarse breadcrumbs.
3. Whisk together egg and milk. Make a well in centre of flour mixture, pour in egg mixture and mix to form a soft dough. Turn onto a lightly floured surface and knead lightly.
4. Press dough out to a 25mm (1in) thickness using the palm of your hand. Cut out scones using a floured 5cm (2in) cutter. Avoid twisting the cutter, or the scones will rise unevenly.
Arrange scones close together on a buttered and lightly floured baking tray or in a shallow 20cm (8in) round cake tin. Brush with a little milk and bake for 12–15 minutes or until golden.

2 cups self-rising (self-raising)
*   flour*
1 teaspoon baking powder
2 teaspoons sugar
45g (1½oz) butter
1 egg
½ cup milk

Date scones

MAKES 12-16

500g (1lb) self-rising (self-raising)
  flour
1 teaspoon salt
2 teaspoons ground cinnamon
60g (2oz) butter
125g (4oz) chopped dates
30g (1oz) sugar
2 cups milk
1 egg
¼ cup milk

1. Preheat oven to 230°C/450°F.
2. Sift flour, salt and cinnamon then, using fingertips, rub butter into the flour mixture. Add dates and sugar. Make a well in the centre and add the milk all at once, stirring quickly and lightly to a soft dough.
3. Turn onto a lightly floured board and knead just enough to make a smooth surface. Pat into 12–18mm (½–¾in) thickness and, using a small scone cutter, cut into rounds.
4. Place on a floured baking tray. Brush tops with combined beaten egg and milk and then bake for about 10 minutes.

Cheese scones

MAKES 12-16

500g (1lb) self-rising (self-raising)
   flour
¼ teaspoon Cayenne pepper
1 teaspoon salt
60g (2oz) butter
1 tablespoon finely chopped
   onion
60g (2oz) Cheddar cheese,
   grated
1 egg
¼ cup parsley, finely chopped
2 cups milk
1 egg, beaten
¼ cup milk

1. Preheat oven to 230°C/450°F.
2. Sift flour, pepper and salt then, using fingertips, rub butter into the flour mixture. Add onion, cheese, egg and parsley. Make a well in the centre and add the milk all at once, stirring quickly and lightly to a soft dough.
3. Turn onto a lightly floured board and knead just enough to make a smooth surface. Pat into 12–18mm (½–¾in) thickness and, using a small scone cutter, cut into rounds.
4. Place on a floured baking tray. Brush tops with combined beaten egg and milk and then bake for about 10 minutes.

Raspberry muffins

1. Preheat oven to 180°C/350°F. Sift dry ingredients into a bowl. Return any bran to the bowl.

2. Beat together buttermilk, orange juice and eggs. Pour into dry ingredients, all at once. Add raspberries and mix until just combined – take care not to overmix. Spoon into buttered muffin pans.

3. Bake for 20–25 minutes or until cooked when tested with a skewer.

1 cup wholemeal self-rising (self-raising) flour

1 cup white self-rising (self-raising) flour

½ cup bran

½ teaspoon baking soda

1 teaspoon ground ginger

¾ cup buttermilk

⅓ cup orange juice concentrate

2 eggs

⅔ cup fresh, or frozen, partly thawed, raspberries

Berry crumble muffins

MAKES 12

1. Preheat oven to 180C°C/350°F. Butter 12 medium muffin tins.
2. In a medium bowl sift together the flours and baking powder and stir in the sugar.
3. In a separate bowl, mix the milk, oil and eggs together. Make a well in the centre of the dry ingredients and pour in the milk mixture.
4. Add the berries and mix until just combined.
5. To make the crumble topping, place the flour and butter in a medium bowl and rub in the butter with your fingertips until the mixture resembles breadcrumbs. Stir in the sugar and set aside.
6. Spoon the dough into muffin tins and sprinkle with the crumble mixture. Bake for 20–25 minutes or until muffins are cooked when tested with skewer. Turn onto wire racks to cool.

1 cup self-rising (self-raising) flour, sifted
1 cup plain flour, sifted
1 teaspoon baking powder
½ cup brown sugar
¾ cup milk
¼ cup canola oil
2 eggs, lightly beaten
1 cup frozen mixed berries

CRUMBLE TOPPING
2 tablespoons plain flour
2 tablespoons brown sugar
30g (1oz) butter, cut into cubes

Carrot muffins

MAKES 12

1½ cups plain flour, sifted
2 teaspoons baking powder
½ teaspoon salt
3 tablespoons sugar
1 teaspoon ground cinnamon
1 teaspoon ground nutmeg
1 cup grated carrot
¼ cup currants
1 egg
½ cup milk
75g (2½oz) butter, melted

1. Preheat oven to 180C°C/350°F. Butter 12 medium muffin tins.

2. In a medium bowl, sift together flour, baking powder, salt, sugar and spices. Mix in grated carrot and currants.

3. Place egg, milk and butter in a small bowl and whisk to combine. Pour milk mixture into dry ingredients and mix with a fork until ingredients are just combined, do not over mix.

4. Spoon mixture into 12 buttered muffin tins. Bake for 20–25 minutes or until muffins are cooked when tested with a skewer. Turn onto wire racks to cool.

Apple scones

MAKES 12

2 cups plain flour
¼ cup granulated sugar
2 teaspoons baking powder
½ teaspoon baking soda
½ teaspoon salt
45g (1¼oz) butter, chilled
1 large apple, peeled and grated
½ cup milk

1. Preheat oven to 220°C/420°F. Combine flour, sugar, baking powder, baking soda and salt in a large bowl. Cut in butter until crumbly.

2. Add apple and milk. Stir to form soft dough. Turn out on lightly floured surface. Knead gently until combined. Pat into two 15cm (6in) circles. Place on buttered baking sheet. Brush tops with milk. Sprinkle with sugar, then with cinnamon. Score each top into six pie-shaped wedges. Bake for 15 minutes until browned and risen. Serve warm with butter.

shortbread

Simple shortbread cookies

MAKES 24

1. Preheat oven to 180°C/350°F.
2. Cream sugar and butter thoroughly. Add the flour and mix well. Turn out onto a lightly floured surface. Knead dough gently until combined. Roll out 6mm (¼in) thick and cut out rounds with cookie cutter. Prick cookies with fork and place on unbuttered cookie sheets.
3. Bake for about 8—10 minutes, or until lightly browned.

1 cup butter
1 cup sugar
2 cups plain flour

Hazelnut shortbreads

MAKES 40

1. Preheat oven to 160°C/325°F.

2. Place butter, flour, hazelnuts and ground rice in a food processor and process until mixture resembles coarse breadcrumbs. Add sugar and process to combine.

3. Turn mixture onto a floured surface and knead lightly to make a pliable dough. Place dough between sheets of baking paper and roll out to 5mm (¼in) thick. Using a 5cm (2in) fluted cutter, cut out rounds of dough and place 25mm (1in) apart on buttered baking trays. Bake for 10—15 minutes or until lightly browned. Stand on baking trays for 2–3 minutes before transferring to wire racks to cool.

4. Place melted chocolate in a plastic food bag, snip off one corner and pipe lines across each biscuit before serving.

250g (9oz) butter, chopped
1½ cups plain flour, sifted
45g (1½oz) hazelnuts, ground
¼ cup ground rice
¼ cup superfine (caster) sugar
100g (3½oz) chocolate, melted

Honey macadamia shortbreads

MAKES 24

½ cup macadamias
1 cup plain flour
½ cup cornflour
¼ teaspoon salt
¼ cup superfine (caster) sugar
125g (4oz) butter
2 tablespoons honey

1. Preheat oven to 200C/400°F.

2. Finely chop half the macadamias. Cut the remainder in half and put aside.

3. Sift flours, salt and sugar together. Rub in the butter until evenly dispersed, stir in the honey and chopped macadamia nuts.

4. Turn onto a lightly floured board and knead lightly. Roll out to 12mm (½in) thickness and place in the refrigerator for about 10 minutes before cutting into rounds using a 5cm (2in) fluted cutter. Place half a nut on each round.

5. Place the shortbreads on a buttered baking tray and bake in the oven for about 15 minutes, or until golden brown.

Chocolate Viennese shortbreads

MAKES 24

250g (8oz) butter
¼ cup superfine (caster) sugar
½ teaspoon vanilla extract
2 tablespoons cocoa powder
1½ cups plain flour
⅓ cup cornflour
150g (5oz) milk chocolate melts,
    melted
confectioners' (icing) sugar, to
    dust

1.   Preheat oven to 180°C/350°F.
2.   Beat butter and sugar together until light and creamy, add vanilla and cocoa and beat until well combined. Fold in sifted flours and spoon mixture into a large piping bag fitted with a large fluted pipe.
3.   Pipe mixture into shapes onto lightly buttered baking trays. Bake for 12–15 minutes then cool on trays.
4.   Dip ends of each biscuit into melted chocolate and set aside to cool until chocolate is set. Dust with icing sugar.

Chocolate shortbread

MAKES 12

1. Preheat oven to 180°C/350°F.
2. Butter and line base and sides of a 20cm x 30cm (8 x 12in) shallow baking pan. Beat butter and sugar in a bowl until pale.
3. Sift in flour, cocoa and baking soda and beat slowly until just combined. Spread in pan and smooth with a spatula. Prick all over with a fork. Chill for 15 minutes.
4. Bake shortbread for 25 minutes or until firm to touch. While it's still hot, use a knife to score it into 12 rectangles.
5. Cool slightly, then remove from pan and cut into 12 pieces. Dust with extra cocoa before serving. Shortbread will keep for 3–4 days in an airtight container.

290g (10oz) unsalted butter
1 cup superfine (caster) sugar
2½ cups plain flour
5 tablespoons cocoa powder
¼ teaspoon baking soda

Hazelnut & Kahlúa shortbreads

MAKES 30

1. Preheat oven to 190°C/375°F.
2. Cream butter and sugar until soft. Add liqueur and hazelnuts and mix well. Fold in sifted flour.
3. Place the mixture into a piping bag fitted with fluted tube, pipe into fancy shapes onto a lightly buttered oven tray.
4. Bake for about 12 minutes or until pale golden brown.

125g (4oz) butter
2 tablespoons confectioners'
    (icing) sugar
2 teaspoons Kahlúa
2 tablespoons ground hazelnuts
¾ cup plain flour, sifted

Choc-mint pinwheels

MAKES 40

100g (3½oz) butter, softened
¾ cup superfine (caster) sugar
1 egg, lightly beaten
1½ cups plain flour
1 teaspoon peppermint essence
2 tablespoons cocoa powder

1. Place butter and sugar in a bowl and beat until light and fluffy. Gradually beat in egg. Add flour and mix to make a soft dough.

2. Divide dough into two equal portions. Knead peppermint essence into one portion and cocoa powder into the other. Roll out each portion of dough separately on non-stick baking paper to make two 18 x 28cm (7 x 11in) rectangles. Place peppermint dough on top of chocolate dough. Roll up from long edge, wrap in cling wrap and chill for 1 hour.

3. Preheat oven to 200°C/400°F. Cut roll into 5mm (¼in) thick slices and place on buttered baking trays. Bake for 8 minutes or until cookies are golden. Transfer to wire racks to cool.

TIP
You may want to add a few drops of green or pink food colouring to the mint-flavoured dough. Chill the rolled dough until quite firm for easier slicing.

Lavender shortbread

MAKES 48

250g (9oz) superfine (caster)
    sugar
2 tablespoons lavender buds
220g (7¾oz) butter, softened
1 teaspoon vanilla extract
300g (10½oz) plain flour
½ teaspoon salt
½ teaspoon bicarbonate of soda

1. Place all the sugar and lavender buds in a food processor and blitz to break up the buds. Transfer the sugar to a covered container and allow to infuse, preferably overnight.

2. Pass the sugar through a sieve to remove the larger bud bits. Combine 220g (7¾oz) sugar, butter and vanilla in a mixing bowl and, using an electric mixer, beat until smooth. In a separate bowl, sift together the flour, salt and bicarbonate of soda. Using a wooden spoon, slowly stir the flour into the butter mixture until smooth. Divide the dough into two balls, cover with clingfilm and chill for 1 hour.

3. Preheat the oven to 190°C/375°F. Lightly grease or line two baking trays with baking parchment.

4. Lightly flour a work surface and roll the balls, one at a time, to 3mm (⅛in) thick. Cut into shapes and sprinkle with the reserved sugar. Transfer to baking sheets. Bake for 8–12 minutes, until very lightly golden. The exact timing will depend on the size of the shapes.

5. Allow to cool on the baking sheets for a few minutes then transfer to wire racks and allow to cool completely.

Brazil nut shortbreads with strawberries

1. Place the nuts and sugar in a food processor and blend until fine. Add the flour and butter and blend until the mixture resembles fine breadcrumbs. Add the egg yolks and pulse until the mixture forms a soft dough, taking care not to over process. Bring the mixture together to form a ball, then wrap in cling wrap and chill for 20 minutes.

2. Preheat the oven to 180°C/350°F. On a lightly floured surface, roll out the dough to 5mm (¼in) thick and stamp out eight 75mm (3in) rounds with a biscuit cutter, re-rolling as necessary. Place on a greased baking tray and bake for 10–12 minutes, until lightly golden. Cool on a wire rack.

3. To make the filling, fold the orange zest into the cream. Place a small amount of cream on each biscuit, top with strawberries, then another biscuit, then more cream and strawberries. Warm the jam in a small saucepan, then drizzle it over the top. Decorate with extra orange zest.

SHORTBREAD
30g (1oz) Brazil nuts
55g (2oz) brown sugar
125g (4oz) plain flour
75g (2½oz) butter, softened
2 medium egg yolks

FILLING
zest of ½ orange
1 cup thickened cream whipped
250g (9oz) strawberries, hulled and sliced
4 tablespoons strawberry jam

Ginger kisses

1. Preheat the oven to 160°C/325°F. Line two baking sheets with baking parchment.
2. In a large bowl beat the butter until pale and creamy. Gradually add the icing sugar, beating well after each addition until the mixture is light and fluffy. Beat in the egg until well combined. If the mixture starts to curdle, add a tablespoon of the flour.
3. In a separate bowl combine the ginger, flour and cornflour. Sift the dry ingredients into the butter mixture and mix thoroughly. Roll teaspoon-sized amounts into balls and press down with a fork.
4. Bake for 20–22 minutes, or until firm and lightly golden in colour. Transfer to a wire rack and allow to cool completely.
5. While the biscuits are cooling prepare the filling. Combine all the ingredients in a bowl and set aside. When the biscuits are cool enough spread the filling on half the biscuits then place the remaining biscuits on top.

250g (9oz) butter, softened
115g (4¼oz) confectioners'
    (icing) sugar, sieved
1 egg, lightly beaten
3 teaspoons ground ginger
225g (8oz) plain flour
150g (5½oz) cornflour

FILLING
250g (9oz) mascarpone
50g (1¾oz) stem ginger, finely
    chopped
1 tablespoon stem ginger syrup
50g (1¾oz) demerara sugar
½ teaspoon vanilla extract

cheesecakes

Pecan cheesecake

SERVES 12

1. Preheat oven to 160°C/325°F.
2. To make base, combine biscuits, sugar and butter, mixing well. Press into bottom of 25cm (10in) springform tin, chill.
3. To make filling, beat cream cheese with an electric mixer until light and fluffy, gradually add brown sugar and butter, mixing well. Add eggs, one at a time, beating well after each addition. Stir in vanilla and pecans. Spoon filling into tin and bake for 1 hour.
4. Turn oven off. Allow cheesecake to cool in oven for 30 minutes. Cool to room temperature then refrigerate for 8 hours. Remove sides of springform tin.
5. Decorate with extra pecans and serve with whipped cream.

BASE
180g (6oz) digestive biscuits, finely crushed
3 tablespoons sugar
50g (1¾oz) butter, melted

FILLING
1¼ kg (2½oz) cream cheese, softened
1⅔ cups light brown sugar, firmly packed
40g (1½oz) butter, melted
5 eggs
1 teaspoon vanilla essence
1 cup pecans, chopped

Classic unbaked cheesecake

SERVES 8

1.   Combine biscuits and butter together and press onto the base of a 22cm (9in) springform tin. Refrigerate while preparing filling.

2.   Cream together the cheese and sugar until smooth. Beat in lemon juice and milk, then gently fold in cream.

3.   Sprinkle the gelatine onto 2 tablespoons hot water and stir briskly until dissolved to a clear golden liquid. Add to cheese mixture.

4.   Whip egg whites until stiff peaks form. Fold into cheese mixture. Pour into prepared tin. Refrigerate until firm.

5.   Decorate with whipped cream and thin lemon twists.

125g (4oz) plain sweet biscuits, crushed
50g (1¾oz) butter, melted
500g (17½oz) cottage cheese or cream cheese
½ cup superfine (caster) sugar
2 tablespoons lemon juice
¼ cup milk
1 cup thickened cream
1 tablespoon gelatine
2 egg whites

Black forest cheesecake

SERVES 10

1½ cups digestive biscuit
  crumbs
60g (2oz) butter, melted
¼ cup cocoa powder
1¾ cups sugar
750g (26½oz) cream cheese
4 eggs
¼ cup amaretto
¼ cup maraschino cherry juice
125g (4oz) semi-sweet
  chocolate, melted
¼ cup sour cream

1. Combine the biscuit crumbs, butter, cocoa and ¼ cup sugar and mix well. Firmly press into the bottom and 25mm (1in) up the sides of a 22cm (9in) springform tin. Set aside.

2. Preheat oven to 180°C/350°F.

3. Beat cream cheese until fluffy with an electric mixer, gradually add remaining sugar and mix well.

4. Add eggs one at a time, beating well after each addition, then add the amaretto and cherry juice until well blended.

5. Pour into crust and bake for 1 hour.

6. When cooked, remove from oven and allow to cool for 2–3 hours on a wire rack.

7. While cake is cooling, combine melted chocolate and sour cream, and when cake is cool, spread evenly over top of cheesecake.

8. Chill in refrigerator overnight. Before serving, garnish with whipped cream and maraschino cherries.

Ricotta cheesecake

SERVES 10

180g digestive biscuits, finely
  crushed
1⅓ kg ricotta, drained
2 cups sugar
8 egg yolks
½ cup plain flour, sifted
zest of 1 lemon
1 teaspoon vanilla extract
8 egg whites
½ cup thickened cream, whipped

1. Preheat oven to 220°C/420°F.
2. Sprinkle a 30cm (12in) springform tin with the biscuit crumbs.
3. Beat ricotta until smooth, gradually add three-quarters of the sugar, then add egg yolks one at a time, mixing well after each addition. Beat in flour, lemon zest and vanilla.
4. Beat egg whites with remaining sugar. Fold whipped cream and egg whites into ricotta mixture and turn into prepared tin. Bake for 10 minutes, lower temperature to 180°C/350°F and bake for 1 hour. Turn off heat and allow to cool in oven with door closed. Dust with icing sugar before serving.

Currant & lemon cheesecakes

SERVES 4

1. Preheat oven to 160°C/325°F.
2. To make base, combine crumbs, butter and sugar. Line four 10cm (4in) springform tins with baking paper, then press mixture evenly onto bottoms of tins.
3. Bake for 5 minutes.
4. To make filling, combine cream cheese, juice, zest and sugar in an electric mixer, mix on medium speed until well combined. Add the eggs one at a time, mixing well after each addition. Stir through the currants, then pour filling over the base.
5. Bake for 25 minutes.
6. To make topping, place the lemon zest in a small saucepan and cover with water. Bring to the boil and simmer for 5 minutes. Drain and rinse the zest. In a small saucepan, combine half the sugar with ½ cup water and bring to the boil, add the zest and simmer for 10 minutes. Meanwhile, place the remaining sugar on a tray. Remove zest from the sugar syrup, strain and dry on absorbent paper. Cool slightly, then roll in the tray of sugar until well coated.
7. Once cooled, remove the cheesecakes from the tins, dust with icing sugar and top with the candied lemon zest.

BASE
60g (2oz) digestive biscuits,
  finely crushed
30g (1oz) butter, melted
¼ cup sugar

FILLING
500g (17½oz) cream cheese,
  softened
2 tablespoons lemon juice
zest of 2 lemons
¼ cup sugar
2 large eggs
½ cup currants

TOPPING
finely grated zest of 2 lemons
1 cup superfine (caster) sugar

Lemon sultana cheesecake

1. Preheat oven to 180°C/350°F.
2. To make base, sift flour, cornflour, custard powder and icing sugar into a large mixing bowl. Rub in butter with your fingers until mixture resembles coarse bread-crumbs. Make a well in the centre of the mixture and stir in egg yolk and enough water to make a firm dough. Wrap in cling wrap and refrigerate for 30 minutes.
3. Roll out pastry to fit the base of a greased 20cm (8in) springform tin. Using a fork, prick pastry base and bake for 10 minutes. Set aside to cool.
4. In a bowl, mix together the sugar, cinnamon and cardamom. Spread evenly over cooled pastry base.
5. To make filling, place cream cheese, yoghurt, sugar, eggs, vanilla and lemon zest in a mixing bowl and beat until smooth. Fold in sultanas.
6. Spoon mixture into prepared base. Bake for 20–25 minutes or until firm. Turn off oven and leave cheesecake to cool in oven with door ajar.
7. To make topping, place cream, lemon juice and zest in a small saucepan and bring to a boil, then simmer, stirring, for 5 minutes or until mixture thickens. Pour topping over cooled cheesecake and chill until required.

BASE
½ cup plain flour
¼ cup cornflour
¼ cup custard powder
1 tablespoon confectioners'
  (icing) sugar
60g (2oz) butter
1 egg yolk
⅓ cup superfine (caster) sugar
1 tablespoon ground cinnamon
1 tablespoon ground
cardamom

FILLING
375g (13oz) cream cheese,
  softened
¼ cup natural yoghurt
½ cup superfine (caster) sugar
2 eggs
1 teaspoon vanilla extract
zest of 1 lemon
170g (6oz) sultanas

TOPPING
½ cup double cream
2 teaspoons lemon juice
zest of ½ lemon

Espresso cheesecake

SERVES 12

1 cup chocolate biscuit crumbs
30g (1oz) butter, melted
1 tablespoon sugar
250g (9oz) bittersweet chocolate,
　chopped
1kg (36oz) cream cheese
1 cup sugar
1 cup sour cream
2 large eggs, plus 2 egg yolks
¼ cup freshly brewed espresso
　coffee
1 teaspoon vanilla extract
1 tablespoon freshly ground
　coffee

GANACHE

1 cup thickened cream
150g (50z) bittersweet chocolate,
　chopped
1 tablespoon instant espresso
　coffee, dissolved in
　2 tablespoons water

1. Preheat oven to 180°C/350°F. Mix together biscuits, butter and sugar in a bowl, then press into the bottom of a 22cm (9in) springform tin. Place in refrigerator while you make the filling.

2. Melt chocolate in the top of a double boiler and set aside to cool. With an electric mixer, cream the cream cheese and sugar until light and fluffy, then add sour cream and mix, ensuring you scrape down the side of the bowl.

3. Add eggs and egg yolks until well mixed, then add espresso, vanilla, ground coffee and melted chocolate until well blended. Scrape down the sides of the bowl and blend mixture another minute to ensure it's well mixed.

4. Pour mixture on to prepared crust, and place springform tin into a water bath. Bake for 45 minutes. Turn off oven and allow to cool for at least 1 hour before removing.

5. While cheesecake is cooling make ganache. In a small saucepan, bring cream to the boil, pour the chopped chocolate over and let stand for 1 minute. Stir to dissolve and then stir espresso into the chocolate mixture.

6. Let ganache cool to room temperature. Pour onto top of cooled cheesecake. Refrigerate for a couple of hours to allow to set.

Guava strawberry cheesecake

SERVES 12

BASE
125g (4oz) plain flour
60g (2oz) butter
1 egg yolk
3 tablespoons lemon juice

FILLING
250g (9oz) ricotta
½ cup natural yoghurt
2 eggs
2 tablespoons lemon juice
60g (2oz) sugar
250g (9oz) strawberries, sliced
100g (3½oz) guava jam

1. To make base, sift the flour into a bowl. Rub in the butter. Add the egg yolk and lemon juice, with a little cold water if required, to make a soft dough. Knead on a lightly floured surface until smooth, then press the dough evenly over the bottom of a 23cm (9in) springform tin. Rest in the refrigerator for 30 minutes.

2. Preheat oven to 190°C/375°F. Cover loosely with baking paper and dried beans. Bake blind for 10 minutes, remove the paper and beans and return to the oven for 5 minutes more. Cool.

3. To make filling, reduce the oven temperature to 180°C/350°F. Beat the ricotta, yoghurt, eggs, lemon juice and sugar in a bowl until smooth. Pour over the pastry base. Bake for 30 minutes or until set, then cool.

4. Purée 100g (3½) of the strawberries in a blender or food processor with the guava jam. Spread over the cheesecake. Place in the refrigerator for 1 hour. Decorate with the remaining strawberries to serve.

Cherry cheesecake

SERVES 12

1. Preheat oven to 135°C/275°F.
2. To make the base, butter a 23cm (9in) springform tin and line with baking paper.
3. Combine biscuit crumbs, sugar, cinnamon and nutmeg and sprinkle evenly over base tin. Set aside.
4. To make the filling, separate eggs and beat yolks until lemon coloured, then gradually add sugar. Cut cream cheese into tiny chunks, beat until smooth, then slowly add egg yolk mixture. Beat until smooth, then add sour cream, flour and vanilla. Beat again until smooth. Beat egg whites until stiff but not dry. Gently fold egg whites into cream cheese mixture. Pour into prepared tin and bake for 1 hour 10 minutes.
5. Turn off heat and leave in oven for 1 hour longer without opening oven door.
6. To make glaze, drain the cherries and place ½ cup of the liquid with the jam and sugar in a saucepan, bring to the boil and reduce by half. Add the cherries and simmer for a further 3 minutes. Cool and pour over the cooled cheesecake.

BASE
60g (2oz) digestive biscuits, finely crushed
1 tablespoon sugar
¼ teaspoon ground cinnamon
¼ teaspoon ground nutmeg

FILLING
5 eggs
1 cup sugar
500g (17½) cream cheese, softened
1 cup sour cream
2 tablespoons plain flour
1 teaspoon vanilla extract

GLAZE
425g (14½oz) canned black cherries
150g (5oz) black cherry jam
½ cup sugar

Rainbow cheesecake

1.   Combine biscuit crumbs and butter and press into the base of a 22cm (9in) springform tin. Soften cheese and beat in sugar. Add vanilla, malt powder and milk, then fold in the cream.

2.   Dissolve gelatine in 2 tablespoons of hot water and add to cheese mixture. Divide mixture into three and place in separate bowls.

3.   To one bowl add the cochineal and to another add the cocoa. Beat egg whites until stiff and fold one-third into each bowl. Pour pink layer onto crust base and smooth.

4.   Gently spoon plain layer on top of the pink layer and smooth. Finally, top with chocolate layer and smooth.

5.   Refrigerate until firm. Decorate with whipped cream and chocolate buttons to serve.

200g (7oz) plain chocolate biscuits, crushed
100g (3½) butter, melted
550g (19oz) cottage cheese
¾ cup superfine (caster) sugar
½ tablespoon vanilla extract
1 tablespoon malt powder
¼ cup milk
1 cup cream
1 tablespoon gelatine
1 teaspoon cochineal (pink colouring)
1 teaspoon cocoa powder
2 egg whites
chocolate buttons to decorate

Spring ice cream cheesecake

SERVES 10

2 cups plain sweet biscuit
    crumbs
170g (6oz) butter, melted
375g (13oz) cream cheese,
    softened
¾ cup superfine (caster) sugar
200g (7oz) fresh or frozen berries
4 cups vanilla ice cream
whipped cream and berries to
    decorate

1. Combine biscuit crumbs and butter in a
bowl and mix well. Press mixture over base
and sides of a 20cm (8in) springform tin and
refrigerate until firm.

2. Beat cheese and sugar together in a
bowl until the mixture is smooth. Blend or
process berries until smooth, then add to
the cheese mixture.

3. Chop up the ice cream, add to the
cheese mixture and beat until smooth.

4. Pour filling on to crust and freeze for
several hours or until firm. Decorate with
whipped cream and fresh berries.

tarts

Princess custard tart

1. Preheat oven to 200°C/400°F. Sift flour and baking powder into butter, salt and sugar and mix with 2 tablespoons cold water to make a firm dough. Roll out pastry to about 6mm and line the base and sides of a greased 20cm (8in) springform tin with the pastry.

2. Make custard by mixing sugar, flour, egg yolks and milk together. Fill the pastry case with the custard mixture.

3. Bake for 25 minutes. While baking, make meringue by beating egg whites with 4 tablespoons sugar.

4. Allow tart to cool then spread thinly with raspberry jam and pile meringue on top. Reduce heat to 120°C/250°F and bake until brown.

175g (6oz) plain flour
1 teaspoon baking powder
90g (3oz) butter
pinch of salt
30g (1oz) sugar
¼ cup raspberry jam

CUSTARD
2 teaspoons sugar
1 teaspoon plain flour
2 egg yolks
1 cup milk

MERINGUE
3 egg whites
6 tablespoons sugar

Apple custard tarts

1. Preheat oven to 180°C/350°F. Combine flour and ½ teaspoon of salt in mixing bowl. Mix in butter until mixture resembles breadcrumbs. Mix in enough cold water to form a firm dough that sticks together, about 6 tablespoons.

2. Shape dough into a ball. Cut in half. Roll out each half on lightly floured surface until 5mm (¼in) thick. Cut 12 circles from each half using fluted biscuit cutter 75mm (3in) in diameter. Fit pastry circles into greased muffin cups, pressing sides so they reach rims.

3. Beat eggs with whisk or electric mixer. Stir in sugar and remaining ½ teaspoon salt. Gradually blend in milk.

4. Spoon one tablespoon crushed apples into each pastry case and then spoon custard mixture over apples until each pastry case is full.

5. Bake until knife inserted in centre of custards comes out clean, about 30 minutes. Remove tarts from muffin cups. Cool on wire racks.

3 cups plain flour
1 teaspoon salt
180g (6oz) butter
3 eggs
⅓ cup granulated sugar
1½ cups milk
400g (14oz) canned pie apples

Mini strawberry custard tarts

MAKES 12

12 frozen mini shortcrust
  pastry cases
2 egg yolks
2 tablespoons superfine (caster)
  sugar
⅓ cup thickened cream
1½ tablespoons strawberry jam
6 small strawberries, hulled
  and halved
1 tablespoon confectioners'
  (icing) sugar

1. Preheat the oven to 160°C/325°F. Place the frozen tart cases on an oven tray and bake for 10 minutes. Remove from the oven and set aside to cool slightly.

2. Meanwhile, whisk the egg yolks and sugar by hand until the sugar dissolves, then stir in the cream.

3. Spread the base of each tart case with ½ teaspoon of strawberry jam. Spoon the egg mixture evenly into each tart case, then bake for 10–12 minutes until the custard is set. When set, take from the oven and place a strawberry half, cut-side down, onto each tart.

4. Leave to cool for 15 minutes, then remove tarts from the foil cases. Place on a platter and dust with icing sugar to serve.

Portuguese custard tarts

MAKES 12

3 sheets frozen puff pastry,
   thawed
1½ cups milk
5 tablespoons cornflour
300g (10½oz) superfine (caster)
   sugar
½ vanilla bean
9 egg yolks

1. Preheat oven to 190°C/375°F. Lightly grease a 12-cup muffin tin and line bottom and sides of cups with puff pastry.

2. In a saucepan, combine milk, cornflour, sugar and vanilla bean. Cook, stirring constantly, until mixture thickens.

3. Place egg yolks in a medium bowl. Slowly whisk half of the hot milk mixture into the egg yolks. Gradually add egg yolk mixture back to remaining milk mixture, whisking constantly.

4. Cook, stirring constantly, for 5 minutes or until thickened. Remove vanilla bean.

5. Fill pastry-lined muffin cups with egg mixture and bake for 25 minutes, or until pastry is golden brown and filling is lightly browned on top.

Lemon & raspberry tart

SERVES 6

1. Preheat oven to 180°C/350°F. Place frozen pastry case on an oven tray – do not remove from the foil tin provided. Scatter the raspberries in the base of the flan case.
2. Beat together the eggs, caster sugar, lemon zest and cream. Strain mixture through a fine sieve and pour over the raspberries. Bake for 30 minutes or until just set.
3. Allow to cool to room temperature, then dust with the icing sugar. Serve with ice cream and raspberries.
4. If using frozen berries, make sure they are thawed – this is important as frozen berries retain excess water which, if it goes into the custard, will increase the volume of liquid and the recipe will not work.

23cm (9in) sweet flan case, frozen
150g (5oz) fresh raspberries
4 eggs
2/3 cup superfine (caster) sugar
zest of 2 lemons
1/2 cup thickened cream
1 tablespoon confectioners' (icing) sugar

Chocolate pear delights

MAKES 6

1. Preheat oven to 200°C/400°F and line 2 oven trays with baking paper. Using a 14cm (6in) plate as a stencil, cut out 2 rounds from each pastry sheet, making a total of 6 rounds. Pierce each pastry round all over with a fork, leaving a 1cm (½in) border, then place on the prepared oven trays.

2. Spread each round with 1–2 tablespoons of melted chocolate, leaving a 1cm (½in) border. Add the sliced pear halves and almond meal to a bowl and gently mix to combine. Divide the pear slices evenly between the pastry rounds and arrange decoratively. Bake for 12–15 minutes.

3. Serve with ice cream, and if you prefer, drizzle with melted chocolate.

4. One of the easiest ways to melt chocolate is to place chopped chocolate in a microwave-safe container and cook on high in 30-second bursts, stirring a little each time until melted.

3 sheets puff pastry, thawed
1 cup milk chocolate buttons, melted
825g (32oz) canned pear halves, drained and sliced thickly
⅓ cup almond meal

Strawberry & cream tartlets

MAKES 4

145g (5oz) plain flour
1 tablespoon superfine (caster)
  sugar, plus extra to dust
100g (3½) unsalted butter,
  softened
finely grated zest of 1 small
  lemon, plus 1 teaspoon juice
½ cup thickened cream
250g (9oz) strawberries, halved
4 tablespoons raspberry or
  redcurrant jam

1. Preheat the oven to 190°C/375°F. Sift the flour and sugar into a bowl. Rub in the butter and the lemon juice and knead lightly until the mixture forms a smooth dough. Cover with cling wrap and refrigerate for 15 minutes.

2. Roll the dough out thinly on a lightly floured surface, divide it into 4 and use it to line four 75mm (3in) loose-bottomed tartlet tins. Line with baking paper and baking beans and bake for 15 minutes. Remove the paper and beans and cook for another 3–5 minutes, until the pastry is golden. Leave to cool for 15 minutes, then remove from the tins.

3. Whip the cream with the lemon zest until it forms soft peaks. Spoon into the cases and top with the strawberries. Melt the selected jam over a gentle heat with 1 tablespoon of water, then press through a sieve and cool slightly. Spoon over the strawberries, then dust with icing sugar and serve.

Apple jam tarts

MAKES 8

250g (9oz) shortcrust pastry
500g (17½oz) apples, peeled
   and cored
juice and zest of 1 lemon
60g (2oz) sugar
30g (1oz) butter
2 eggs, lightly beaten
⅓ cup blackberry jam

1. Preheat oven to 200°C/400°F. Line 8 patty tins with the pastry, prick with a fork and cook for about 10–15 minutes, until browned. Cook the apples with water for 15 minutes.

2. When cooked, rub through a sieve, return to the saucepan and add lemon zest, juice, sugar, butter and eggs. Allow to cook over a low heat until the mixture thickens slightly.

3. Place a teaspoon or two of the jam in the bottom of each pastry case and then fill the cases with the apple mixture and return to oven to set. Serve sprinkled with sifted icing sugar.

Easy chocolate tart

1. Lightly grease the base of a 20cm (8in) springform tin.

2. Combine crushed biscuits and butter in a bowl. Press mixture into base of tin. Chill for 30 minutes until set.

3. Combine milk and dark chocolate in a microwave-safe bowl. Melt on medium (50%) power for 1 minute. Stir and return to oven for 30 seconds. Continue cooking in this way until melted and smooth. Mix in icing sugar. Set aside to cool slightly.

4. Fold cream through chocolate. Pour over biscuit base. Smooth top and chill for 5 hours or overnight, until set. Melt white chocolate, pipe or drizzle over tart and serve.

200g (7oz) plain sweet biscuits, crushed
100g (3oz) butter, melted
150g (5oz) milk chocolate, roughly chopped
150g (5oz) dark chocolate, roughly chopped
2 tablespoons confectioners' (icing) sugar, sifted
1¼ cups thickened cream, whipped
50g (1¾) white chocolate

Homeland jam tart

1. Preheat the oven to 200°C/400°F.
2. Line a baking tray with baking paper, place a ring mould onto the tray. Cut a large round from the pastry and use to line the base and sides of the mould to form a tart case. Trim the excess pastry. Bake blind for 6–8 minutes or until the pastry is light golden.
3. Place the raspberries and sugar in a bowl, add the lemon juice and microwave for 6–8 minutes on high (100%) or until thickened and jam-like.
4. Remove the mould from the pastry case. Spoon the jam into the pastry case and allow to cool before serving. Dust with icing sugar and serve with whipped cream.

1 sheet shortcrust pastry
1½ cups frozen raspberries
½ cup superfine (caster) sugar
juice of ½ lemon

Berry tarts

MAKES 4

1 sheet puff pastry, thawed
3 cups fresh berries
1½ tablespoons caster or
   brown sugar
1 tablespoon milk

1. Preheat oven to 200°C/400°F and line an oven tray with baking paper. Cut pastry into quarters and place on the prepared oven tray. In a small saucepan over a medium-low heat, cook the berries with the sugar for 2 minutes until soft. Strain through a sieve and reserve the liquid. Divide mixture evenly between pastry squares, then roll edges of pastry in to form a 10cm round shape. Brush pastry edges with milk and scatter with a little extra sugar.

2. Bake for 15 minutes or until crisp and golden brown. Use reserved liquid to decorate the serving plate by pouring a thin circle around the edge of each plate.

3. Serve with vanilla yoghurt or vanilla ice cream.

Raspberry & hazelnut tarts

MAKES 6

1 cup flour, sifted
2 tablespoons confectioners'
   (icing) sugar
30g (1oz) hazelnuts, ground
80g (2½oz) unsalted butter,
   chopped
1 egg, lightly beaten

CREAM FILLING
375g (13oz) cream cheese
2 tablespoons superfine (caster)
   sugar
¼ cup double cream

RASPBERRY TOPPING
350g (12oz) raspberries
⅓ cup raspberry jam, warmed
   and sieved

1.   To make pastry, place flour, confectioners' (icing) sugar and hazelnuts in a bowl and mix to combine. Rub in butter, using fingertips, until mixture resembles fine breadcrumbs. Add egg and mix to form a soft dough. Wrap in cling wrap and refrigerate for 1 hour.

2.   Preheat oven to 200°C/400°F. Knead pastry lightly, then roll out to 3mm (1/8in) thick and line six lightly buttered 75mm (3in) flan tins. Line pastry cases with baking paper and weigh down with uncooked rice and bake for 10 minutes. Remove paper and rice and bake for 15 minutes longer or until golden. Set aside to cool.

3.   To make filling, place cream cheese and sugar in a bowl and beat until smooth. Beat cream until soft peaks form then fold into cream cheese mixture. Cover and chill for 20 minutes.

4.   To assemble, spoon filling into pastry cases and smooth tops. Arrange raspberries over top of tarts, then brush warm jam over raspberries and refrigerate for a few minutes to set glaze.

Index

Picture credits
Copyright rests with the following photographers and/or their agents.

Front cover and p4: iStock,
p2-3,p5,p6,p7,p8,p23,p41,p65,p83,p101,p119,p141,and p165: Shutterstock.

First published in 2013 by
New Holland Publishers
London • Sydney • Cape Town • Auckland
www.newhollandpublishers.com

Garfield House 86–88 Edgware Road London W2 2EA United Kingdom
1/66 Gibbes Street Chatswood NSW 2067 Australia
Wembley Square First Floor Solan Road Gardens Cape Town 8001 South Africa
218 Lake Road Northcote Auckland New Zealand

A catalogue record of this book is available at the British Library and the National Library of Australia.

ISBN: 9781742573779

Managing Director: Fiona Schultz
Publishing: Lliane Clarke
Design: Lorena Susak
Production Director: Olga Dementiev
Printer: Toppan Leefung Printing Limited

10 9 8 7 6 5 4 3 2 1

Follow New Holland Publishers on
Facebook: www.facebook.com/NewHollandPublishers